I can't hear the Walls

by
Marilyn Maple, Ph.D

illustrated by
Andrea Johnson

author © Marilyn Maple 2009 * illustration & design © Andrea Johnson 2009

Order this book online at www.trafford.com
or email orders@trafford.com

Most Trafford titles are also available at major online book retailers.

Printed in Victoria, BC, Canada.

ISBN: 978-1-4269-2892-5 (sc)

ISBN: 978-1-4269-2893-2 (e-book)

Library of Congress Control Number: 2010902926

*Our mission is to efficiently provide the world's finest, most comprehensive book publishing
service, enabling every author to experience success. To find out how to publish your book, your
way, and have it available worldwide, visit us online at www.trafford.com*

Trafford rev. 3/11/2010

Trafford PUBLISHING® www.trafford.com

North America & international
toll-free: 1 888 232 4444 (USA & Canada)
phone: 250 383 6864 ♦ fax: 812 355 4082

I can't hear *the*
Walls

by

Marilyn Maple, PhD

...and illustrated by

Andrea Johnson

This book is dedicated to
the members of our critique group
who readily recognize the
flaws in human endeavor:
Joan and Jay Carter,
Leonard Emmel,
Carrie Dukes, Mary Glazer,
Dan Malachoff, Frances Ogle,
Liz Smith, Joan Froede, Jim Minic,
Art Crummer and Skipper Hammond

Introduction

Truth is vision.
Knowledge expands thought.
Wisdom gives insight
To find truth within,
One must have the vision
And the insight to find
Beauty in all things.
This is enlightenment.

Diversity

We are vessels formed by the clay of life.
None of us is perfect.
Each of us is flawed either by birth, life,
circumstance, disease or distress.

Whether created by a Master Creator

Evolution

Chemistry

or

Genetics

and

Whether our living being is sculpted through

Nature or Nurture...

Imperfection and anomaly

ARE THE NATURE OF BEING.

This book attempts to bring to light
the beauty in the diversity of all human beings
as we struggle to survive, cope, and realize our dreams.

I WAS BORN TO BE...

A little child with eyes...

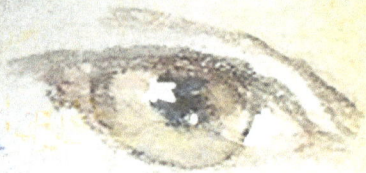

here   and   here

with a nose that spread
out to here...

and ran into my mouth...

so that I had a hard time eating and drinking and talking and
looking pretty and cute to my mother and dad and my family.

My name is Nancy.

When I was born, some people thought I looked like a monster.
Even my parents were disappointed in me so they sent me to a
special place that took care of people who were not like most people.

Eventually they put me up for adoption.
Even in this hospital-kind of home, the people
looked at my face and thought that if my face was
so misshapen, my mind must also be distorted,
just like my face. They said I would have to have
lots of operations, but there was no money.
They told me I would never learn because
my mind must be slow and filled with sadness.
Someone said I was like a little bird
with a broken wing that would never fly.

One of the attendants didn't believe this about me. She looked
into my eyes and saw behind them, a little girl who understood
what everyone said and who desperately wanted to get out
and be a part of the world. She taught me to believe, to hope, to dream.

I believed that I could learn, even go to school, and maybe college.
I hoped I could find a family that would love me. I dreamed that someday
I might be able to have the operations that would make me look human
and my biggest dream was to fall in love and be loved by someone.

She helped me to accept myself no matter how I looked.
She loved me enough to take time to find a foster family
who took me into their hearts. I was placed in school
and had to catch up with the others.
I couldn't make them understand
because of my mouth; my speech
was distorted. But I tried.

Life looked so much better outside the hospital.
I believed, I had hope...
I even had a family...
but what about the rest of my dreams?

I WAS BORN TO BE...
A dark haired little Mexican girl
with big beautiful brown eyes
that couldn't see.

My name is Karla.

I was born in Nogales, Mexico.
My family loved me very much
and tried to make sure
I had everything
to make my life important.

Because there were no
schools for the blind,
they had to adopt me out
to a family in the United States
so that I could attend a school
for the blind and deaf.
It was a wonderful school
and I loved my classmates.
On weekends I would go back
and visit my real parents.
They would provide me with
all kinds of things to do
to help me realize
I could live a normal life.

Our life was very normal, just like the American children,
I watched television, even though I couldn't see.
I could see with my fingers so I could learn what people
looked like. My ears could see too. At school I hated rainy
days because I couldn't hear the walls.

You see, when I walked down the corridors at school I could
hear where the wall ended and I knew I could turn into
another corridor. It was kind of like a sonar or vibration.
But on rainy days, it was impossible to hear the walls.

I learned a lot. I wrote on a computer that could print out
in print or braille. My fingers learned to read braille,
but as I learned more and more, I also dreamed
more and bigger dreams.

When my teacher asked me what I wanted to be,
I told her I wanted to write and produce television programs.
She didn't laugh at me.
She did ask me how I thought I could do that. I didn't know,
I just felt that somehow I could do it, if I really tried.
I realized that I didn't know what things looked like
- a blue sky...*what was blue*, a sunset, a tree, a bird?

Just like a bird, my dreams took off, my imagination flew
into a make believe future, *that might never come true.*

I BECAME...
what others call disabled.

My name is Dedier.

I was born in Angola,
on the continent of Africa.
My mother was from
French West Africa,
my father was from Angola.

Africa was changing and countries
were adopting new names
and borders were changing
and people were on the move
to avoid war and famine.
We lived in a small compound.

We didn't have to move but all around us people were begging
and walking along the roads, trying to get somewhere.
Our compound was on the edge of an area that once had been the
scene of fighting. It hadn't been too long ago when two tribes of
Angolans, who didn't like each others leaders, fought to the death
right here near our compound.
Of course, we didn't live there then.

My mother and father had gone to Zaire to avoid the fighting.
When they began fighting in Zaire they moved back to Angola
where the fighting had moved on to another place.

One day I was playing along
the edge of the compound.
It was a sunny day and I was
following my friend into the edge
of the jungle that surrounded the compound.
We were pretending to look for tigers.

Suddenly, there was a loud boom. I found myself
on the ground. There was blood all around.
My people were standing over me.
It was a long time before before I could
look down and find, I no longer had my legs.
It was difficult for me to think I would never walk...
never hunt tigers...
but in my dreams, I still walked, I still ran.

Thank goodness for dreams.

I SEE...
everything in the world...
but I hear...
nothing.

My name is Odessa,
although I didn't know my name.

I was abandoned by my mother
and was taken to many places.
Places where I lived with other children.
The children would come up to me
and move their lips.

But I didn't know what they were doing.
I didn't know what anything was.
At the places they took me
I had a little place to lie down
and when I could look outside,
there were big forms outside my window.

They had round bottoms, made of rough pieces
of something and as they got taller,
they had little arms that were covered
in thin little forms that waved in the air.

In my head I began to place everything I saw in visual categories.

Every year I would move. Sometimes I moved more than once.
I always knew when I was going to a different place
because they would pack my clothes and a big bus
would come to take me along with other children.

One day the bus came. It didn't look like the other buses
but they had packed my clothes and I was put on the bus.
I didn't want to leave. I didn't want to go to some place new.
The children on the bus came up to me but instead
of moving their lips they moved their fingers in front of my face.
I wasn't sure whether they liked me.

When the bus stopped the children ran off. I stayed on.
I didn't want to leave. The driver tried to get me off but
I had a sharp thing they use to cut up food and I waved it at him.
Then a young man with a nice smile came on the bus.
He moved his fingers at me. I waved the sharp thing.
He touched my hand and his touch was gentle.
He touched my cheek and stroked it.
 I gave him the sharp thing and we got off the bus together.

There were little houses all around and a big, big bathtub of water
with those big tall things I used to see outside my window,
but here there were lots of them. I watched the others play
and wished I could know what they were doing with their fingers.
I wondered if someday I would know what everything I saw was
...maybe it was just a dream.

I BECAME...
a patient in a hospital in Bosnia.
We were having a terrible war
and everyone was getting killed
...even the children.

My name is Anya.

I was running down a street
when a man with a gun
turned the corner
at the same time I did
and he hit me with the gun.
I was very little and it did
something to my head.
When I woke up,
I was in a hospital, in a bed.

I began to shake all over.
Then I don't remember
anything for a while.
The next I remember is
my mother bending over me.
She was talking to a doctor
who said I had "seizures".
He said my brain was damaged.
I didn't know what this meant.
I just knew that lots of times
during the day, I would start to shake
and then I wouldn't open my eyes
for a while and when I did,
I was weak and I ached all over.
It was scary.

I heard the hospital people talk
and they said there was nothing
they could do for me.
Every day I just lay there.
Every day was just the same.
Every day. Every day.

Then one day the nurses
gathered around me.
They whispered together.
Should they tell me,
or shouldn't they tell me
that my mother was dead.

I wanted to be with my mother.
I dreamed of being with my mother.
I dreamed the war was over.
I dreamed I was who I used to be.

I FELT...
the dry wind against my skin.

It was the same wind that touched the faces of my ancestors.
I knew I carried their spirit in me but as a very young boy,
I kept searching among the rocks and canyons
trying to find their spirit to capture it for myself.

My name is White Cloud.

I am Navajo. I am a very proud Navajo.
We are a great tribe and we take care of each other.
Also, I must tell you, that I am a different Navajo.
I am what they call "albino".

I can live this way, but people stare at me
and I feel as if I am not a part of real life.
That's why I walk out into the desert to see
if I can capture the spirits of my ancestors.

Albino.
That means I do not have
the red skin of my tribe.
My skin is very white.
My hair is not black, it is white.
That is why they called me White Cloud.
My eyes are also not like the others.
They tell me my eyes are blue and pinkish.
I do not know because my sight is very poor.
I can see some things,
like the canyons and the cactae.

My tribe is very nice to me.
They encouraged me
to go to a school
especially for the blind.
I must admit I thought that maybe
they wanted me to leave because
I was a disgrace to the tribe being so white.

I went to school. I learned.
I have no dreams
because I have no spirit.
Without spirit you cannot dream.

I FELT...
angry.

My name is Chris.

I did not want to be "socialized"
but my parents
and the psychologist
said I should be.

They mainstreamed me
into a regular school
so that I would be
with normal kids.
This was to make me
more acceptable
as a human being.

I did not want people.
I liked being alone in my mind.

One September when I went back to school
we had a new teacher. His name was Peter.
He started by reading us the story of Peter Pan.

I liked Peter Pan. He was like me.
He could fly away from anything
when he wanted to. All the other people
in the world were Captain Hooks.
They always had their hooks out
to trap me into learning.

Then one day our teacher asked if we
would like to put on a play about Peter Pan.
Some of the other children said "yes".
I had a hard time saying "yes".
That night when I went to sleep
I dreamed I was Peter Pan. I was very good.

Then in class, the teacher suggested to each one
what role he thought would be good for us to play.
He assigned Tiger Lilly, and Wendy to the girls.
He assigned one of the boys to Smee
and he said he would play Captain Hook.
Then he came to me and asked me if I would
play the part of Peter Pan.
I didn't know what to say.
It meant I had to learn lines and
learning things in order was difficult.
I didn't want to be laughed at;
I wasn't sure.

I EXIST...
in a tunnel of time.
I am alive, for now.
I am a girl.
I don't dream.
I don't wish.

I don't know who my mother was
but I was hurt either when I was
inside of her or when I was born.
Something inside my head wasn't right.
It was damaged. I have something
they call cerebral palsy.
I can't remember things very long
but if someone helps me,
I can often remember.

My name is Brandi.

I was placed with a group
of children like myself.
Children that weren't able
to live in the world.
I can remember
that I couldn't walk.
I never really wanted to walk.
Wanting takes thinking.
I never dreamed I could walk.
Dreaming means you have to
hold a thought for a long time
and I can't do that.

I don't even wish for anything
because I live from one minute to another.

One day a man and woman
came to see me.
I enjoyed the moments they were with me.
Later they became my guardians.
I call them my guardian angels.

They said that doctors
someday might find a way to help me.
If they find ways to help me,
I might someday become a "maybe" girl
where I could hold a thought
that let me think that "maybe"
I could do things I can't do now.

I HAVE LEARNED TO EXIST...

My name is Jeremy.

I live in a step-by-step,
day by day world...
but I'm still alive.

I was diagnosed with cancer
when I was eleven.
I was a very good student.

They gave me medicine
that was supposed to
help me get rid of the cancer,
but it didn't.

I learned then that
I had to love my cancer
because it was a part of me,
and if I didn't love all of me,
I wouldn't get well.

So I learned to love my cancer
as something that was meant
to be a part of me.

They decided to give me the medicine
through a tube in my head.
That was successful.
I went into remission.

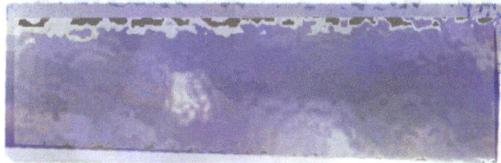

The after effect of the medicine
made me lose certain brain functions.
My memory wasn't very good
but I learned how to make lists
and that helped a lot. I was also told
that I probably would not be able
to father children but that was all right
because I was an adopted child
so I knew that I could adopt other children.

When I was in my twenties, I suffered a stroke.
I couldn't move my legs and was in a wheel chair.
I needed care every day.

I figured, I had to learn to love my stroke
since it was a part of me;
just like the cancer.

All life lends richness to the universe.
The sharing of dreams
is one of life's greatest gifts.
Dreams do come true.

I am smiling at you.
Nancy (19 years old)

I had 23 operations that made my face look pretty normal
and I was pleased when I looked in the mirror.
I learned to speak so that I could be understood.

I even speak before audiences and tell them
what it is like to be born with facial distortions
and how much time it takes to learn
to speak if you have a cleft palate.

I went to school and graduated from high school.
I am going to a community college
and expect to graduate in the normal time.

Just before I went to college my original family
wanted to see me. I had a very hard time
with deciding how I felt about that. After all, they left me.
I finally decided to see them. They were complete strangers
to me but they were nice and tried hard to explain
to me why they had put me in the home.
I listened and I could hear that they were really sorry.
I decided that there was little reason for me to feel resentful.
I was being given the opportunity to have two families.
That's what I have today. Both families are mine
and we all get along very well together.

All my dreams have come true
because now I have a steady boy friend
and we love each other and hope to be married.

This little bird's wing took a long time to heal,
but now, I'm flying.

Let it rain... let it rain.
There are no walls.
Karla (21 years old)

As my senior project in the School for the Deaf and Blind
I wrote a video script and other members of my class
who had low level seeing video taped the script.
They also did the video editing while I edited the audio.
It was a good video based on the music 'You are My Hero'.

I applied to the University and told them
I wanted to major in communications,
in particular, the production of television .
They sounded a bit skeptical as if I couldn't do it.
I showed them my production and they gave me a chance.

This year I graduate with my
bachelor's degree in Mass Communications.

I still don't know what a bird looks like...
but I know how it feels to fly.

Hey, get a load of me!
I am happy to be *Dedier*
(12 years old)

I learned how to lift myself and scoot
around the compound without my legs.
Life wasn't quite the same as standing up
but I was able to play
and learned to use my hands well.
I had no hope that I would ever walk again.

One day a group of people from another country
came to visit our compound.
They were particularly interested
in the children who had lost their arms and legs
because of mines hidden long ago by soldiers.
That's how I lost my legs.
There were lots of us so we had learned
to accept each other's losses.

Some of the people in the group were doctors
who said we could get something they called a "prosthesis".
I didn't know what that was but they explained
through an interpreter that it meant artificial legs and arms.
That's when I started to dream that someday I would walk.

The group went away but some of them
came back months later and fitted me
and some of my friends with legs and arms.

They felt strange at first,
but no more strange
than it felt to lose
your arms and legs.

The first day I took a step,
I knew my dream had come true.

Language is everything!
Odessa (16 years old)

One day as I was sitting under the big curved thing,
a girl came up to me and wiggled her fingers
and pointed to herself. Then she wiggled her fingers
at me and pointed at me. I saw something different.
She did it again.

This time I saw that her fingers moved differently
when she pointed to me. I realized that what her fingers said
when she pointed to me was who I was.
Then I realized that what her fingers said
when she pointed to herself was who she was.

At that moment, a big world opened up to me.
The kids and the adults began teaching me sign language.

The big curved things I saw had names.
They were trees and different kinds of trees with different names.
I learned to swim in the big bathtub which I learned was a lake.
I learned that I was at a camp for the deaf.

On the last night of camp I was very sad
because I had made so many friends.
That night they gave out awards
for the best swimmers and runners and crafts
but the biggest award they gave
was one they called the Miss Congeniality award
and that they gave to me.

When I went home, I spent a lot of time
sitting under the trees and I think
about my summertime friends
and the language that they taught me.

Somebody really wanted me...
do you believe?
Anya (10 years old)

I lay in my bed day after day.
One day a lady and a man came
and looked at all the children.
They paused at my bed
but I didn't look at them.
They moved around
and talked to all the children.
Then they came back to me
and the lady took my hand.
I looked at her then.

What seemed a long time later the same people
came and I was wrapped up and taken with them
on a plane to a new home, a new land.
I didn't know what was happening.
Lots of doctors came to look at me
and they gave me some medicine to take.
I got special food and they did an operation on my head
so that I don't have as many seizures anymore.

The man and woman adopted me
and became my new mother and father.
At night I close my eyes
and I can still see my mother's face,
but when I open my eyes,
I see a whole new world
...a world where I can dream
and maybe they will come true.
I don't want to die
and go to live with my mother anymore.
I want to live with my new family.

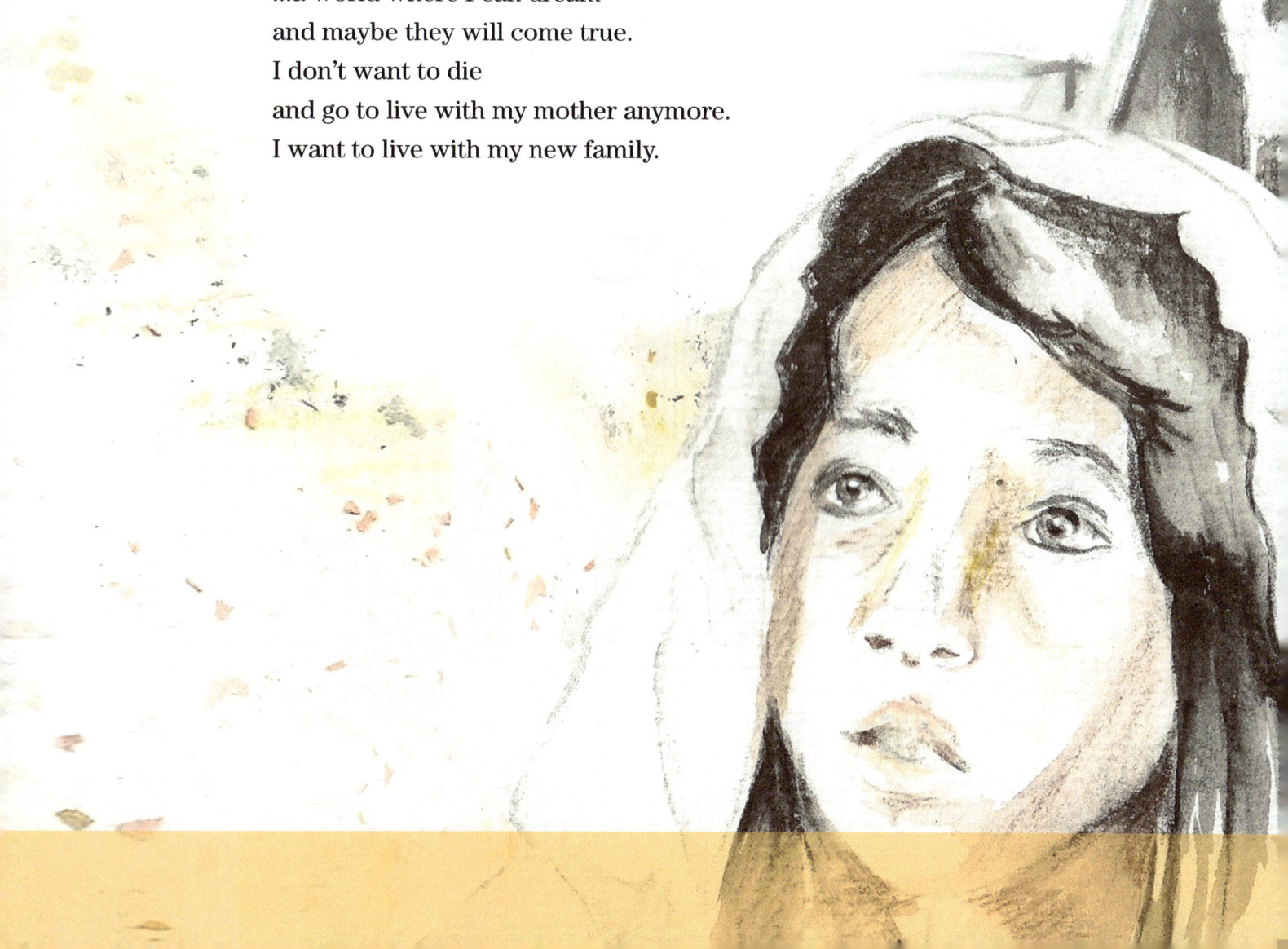

I have the spirit.
White Cloud
(16 years old)

After I graduated from the School for the Blind,
I went home to the reservation.
Everyday I went out to the hills
of my ancestors to ask them why I was living
and what I was supposed to do.

One day while I was standing on a sacred hill
a huge white cloud appeared. I watched it
get larger and larger until it seemed to
wrap itself around me.
Then I heard a voice that said:
"You are special, White Cloud.
You must not be sad
that you are not like the others.
You have a special mission,
you must teach others that
although their hair is different,
and their skin a different color
we are all the same.

We all dream dreams and we all need to have
the opportunity to make them come true.
You must teach others to see with their hearts.
Then the cloud burst and there was rain".

I cried.

I am now planning to go to college
to become a teacher of children...
all kinds of children.

I know what it feels like to play!
Chris (14 years old)

Our class was called
a special education class
in a middle school.
The "normal" students didn't have
much to do with us.
When they heard we were going to
be putting on a play about Peter Pan,
instead of laughing at us,
they came to help us.
They helped make costumes
and when it came to scenery,
we all painted it together.
It didn't matter
if we made mistakes.

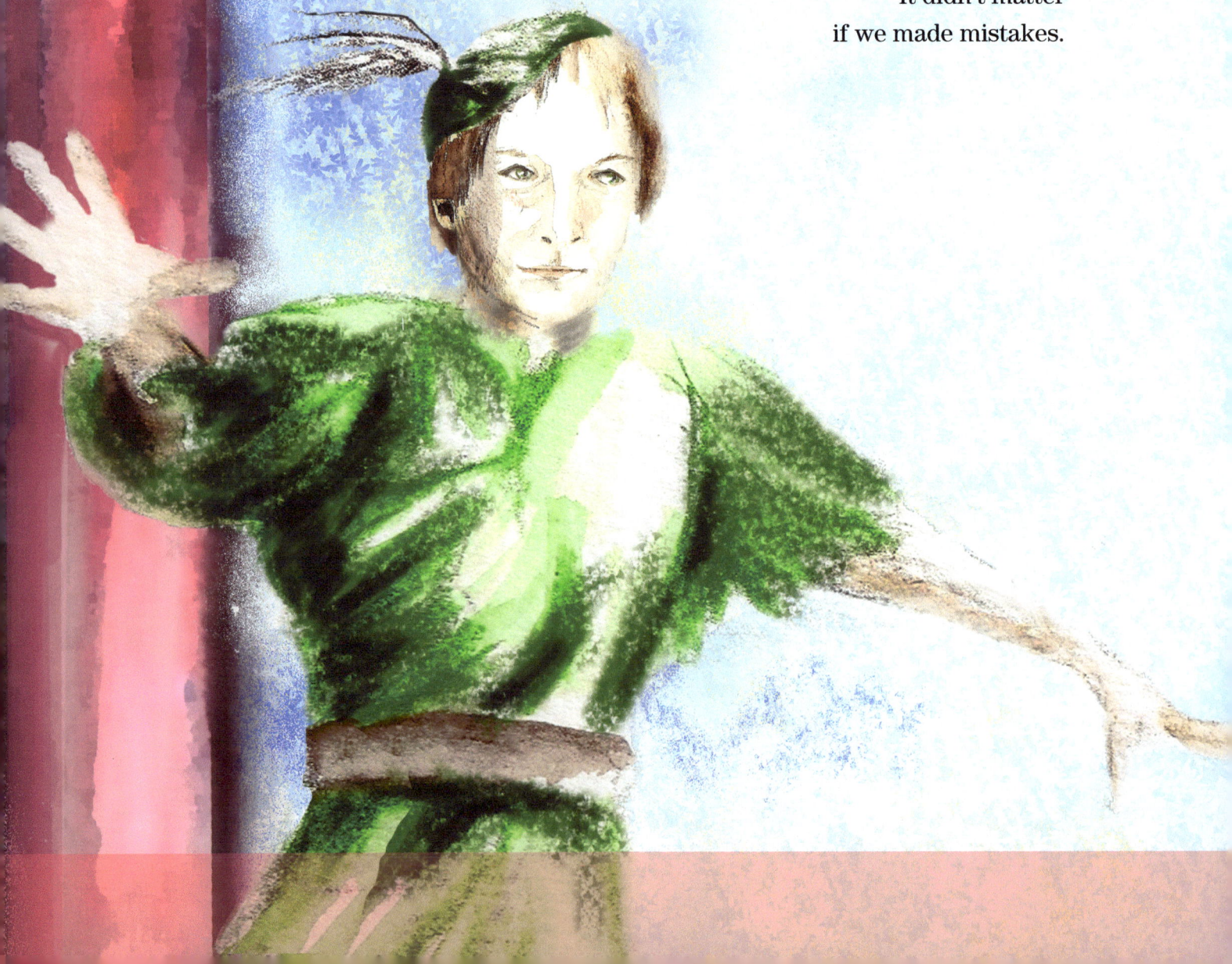

I liked all of that,
but I couldn't learn my lines.
I yelled at my teacher,
"I DON'T WANT TO BE PETER PAN."
He just smiled at me as if
he could look inside of me
and knew I wanted very much
to be Peter Pan.
I didn't like him knowing me that well.
I like my insides to be just for me.
We practiced.
We all had trouble learning lines.
Then the teacher said,
"you don't have to learn each word...
you just have to say
what you think your character
would say in the situation."
That made me feel better
because I really knew
the story of Peter Pan.

Finally, the day came
when the sheet curtains parted
and we put on the play.
I was Peter Pan.
I did very well because
all the people applauded
at the end and whistled and yelled.

Our teacher video-taped the play. The next day he played it.
I saw myself. I liked being Peter Pan because, I like to fly.
That was the best day of my life.

Setting goals
is good for me
and so is
medical technology.
Brandi (14 years old)

I am a "maybe" girl now...
because I learned to say
"maybe" I will walk... and I did.

Then I said "maybe" I can go
to regular school even though
it is special education.
I was tested – I could go to school.
I did that. I went to regular school.

Now I am saying "maybe"
in about three years
I can live with girls like myself
in our own apartment.

That's a big "MAYBE".

But there's that bigger maybe.
Maybe with all the great minds
working to find cures
through medicine and technology,
like special scans, they will be able to
see my brain and where it is hurt
and MAYBE someday
they will be able to fix my brain...
then I will become a think for yourself girl.
I'll be a girl, *able to dream.*

I licked it through love.
Jeremy (24 years old)...

I learned to love my stroke
because only since I had the stroke
did I really know
how wonderful it was to walk.
Through physical therapy
some of my muscles came back.
I had problems with my hands too
but then one day my parents
gave me a computer.
It was so important for me
to be able to use the computer
that I worked very hard
to manage my fingers.

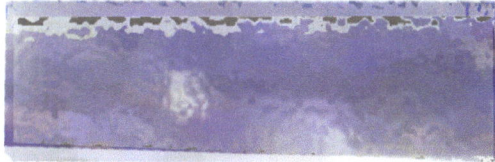

I finally learned and now, every day I am in touch with other children who have some of the same difficulties. We don't call them problems because we realize that what we struggle to do makes us who we are.

I am now sharing an apartment with some others guys who are blessed with some unique abilities.

We love ourselves and we dream.

I still dream about having a wife and some adopted children.
I know that dreams come true.

Each human vessel is unique and imperfect.

It is our "maybe"s and our dreams that turn
inadequacies into works of art.

The broken wing is healed...
the bird flies
and...
there are no walls.

We are our dreams
body, mind and spirit...

And as we dream,

we stand on the shoulders of

those imperfect beings who have gone before us

and shown us the way to beauty and truth...

ABOUT THE AUTHOR

Marilyn Maple, Ph.D. is retired from the University of Florida where for 30 years she produced educational media for six medically related colleges.

Her first children's book, "On the Wings of a Butterfly", was written at the request of terminally ill children who wanted to know about dying. This book is in its second printing and has found a home in Hospices and Aids Clinics. The book is published by Parenting Press, Seattle, Washington.

Her second children's book, "The Refuge" was written about a retirement village for wild animals. In this book she addresses the problems of the animals, all of whom demonstrate human disabilities or problems, such as a lion who has a cleft palate and lisps when he roars, a bengal tiger who suffers depression because his sister died, and an albino skunk who was not acceptable to his family because he was white and different. This book and her third book "Two Bunny Tails" was published by Trafford Publishing, Victoria, Canada.

THE ILLUSTRATOR

Andrea Johnson is a graphic artist working on the Gold Coast Hinterland of Australia. It's almost a full circle for her, as she began her career in the medical profession caring for children...many of whom were very similar to the characters Marilyn has brought to life in *I can't hear the Walls*.

After raising three beautiful daughters and years of harbouring the desire to develop her creative nature, a few years ago Andrea took the big step towards becoming an independant illustrator. With several years under her belt, she now works full time as an artist.

Dreams have come true for Andrea too!